Getting Things Done
secrets
The experts tell all!

About the author

Rus Slater is a management consultant and trainer in the UK who has worked in many areas of industry, commerce and public service. He is also a Course Director for Time Manager International and the author of *Team Management* and *People Management*, also in the **business secrets** series.

Author's note

This book is dedicated to Margaret Ellen Slater (1922–2009)

Getting Things Done
Secrets

Collins

A division of HarperCollins*Publishers*

77-85 Fulham Palace Road, London W6 8JB

www.BusinessSecrets.net

First published in Great Britain in 2010 by HarperCollins*Publishers*
Published in Canada by HarperCollins*Canada*. www.harpercollins.ca
Published in Australia by HarperCollins*Australia*. www.harpercollins.com.au
Published in India by HarperCollins*PublishersIndia*. www.harpercollins.co.in

1

ISBN 978-0-00-734111-5

Printed and bound at Clays Ltd, St Ives plc

Contents

Getting things done is the way to get on in life

If you want to get on in your career or your home life you will need to get things done. In the modern world, however, there are lots of different people wanting lots of different things to be done, and you can't do everything for everyone unless you get much better at a number of different things.

I've been working for over 15 years with individuals and organizations to help them to find ways of getting more done. This ranges from teams with enormous workloads and tight deadlines to individuals simply looking to improve their productivity. I've learned many secrets and tricks over the years. Some I've discovered myself, but many I've learned from others; humans are wonderfully inventive.

This book aims to help you to get better at managing your life to allow you to get more of the things done that you need to get done. It contains 50 **secrets**, grouped into seven themed chapters. If you follow the secrets you will find that you amaze yourself at how much you can actually achieve!

"If we did all the things we are capable of doing we would truly astound ourselves"

Thomas Edison (1847–1931), American inventor

The seven themed chapters are:

■ **Knowing what things to do.** You need to know what it is that needs to be done. You also need to be happy that you are doing the 'right' thing.

■ **Knowing how to do things.** Sometimes you have to do things in a way that is laid down by the organization; other times it is up to you.

■ **Knowing when to do things.** You aren't likely to have just one thing to do – you probably have loads, so you need to know how to prioritize tasks.

■ **Working to your plan.** You know what and how you want to work, but people keep distracting you. How do you manage distractions so that you can get things done?

■ **Saying "no".** You could get it all done if only people wouldn't keep asking you to do other things. You need to learn when to say "no".

■ **Dealing with problems.** You thought you could do that job in an hour, but something has gone wrong. Here's how to prevent and solve these problems.

■ **Asking others to do things.** Sometimes the best way to do something is to get someone else to do it for you. This shows how you can successfully enlist the help of other people.

Learn the secrets of planning, prioritizing and managing workloads.

Knowing what things to do

Firstly it is critically important to recognize that you are responsible for your own destiny. This chapter aims to help you set out your personal mission or vision, to recognize the value of using your time wisely and to develop some foundation strategies to help you manage your time. You need to ensure that the things you do are of value both to you and to your organization.

1.1

Check your bank balance of time

Imagine you have an account at a bank where you automatically get credited each morning with $86,400. Every evening the bank takes back whatever part of the balance you failed to spend during the day. Nothing can be carried over or transferred. What would you do? Well, I'd try to spend every cent, and I bet you would too!

You do have such a bank account; at the 'Bank of Time'. Every morning, it credits you with 86,400 seconds. Every night it debits whatever portion of this total you have failed to invest to some 'good' purpose.

"The Future is something which everyone reaches at the rate of sixty minutes an hour, whatever he does, whoever he is" C.S. Lewis, English author

"Dost thou love life? Then do not squander time, for time is the stuff life is made of."

Benjamin Franklin (1706–90), a Founding Father of the USA

If you fail to use the day's deposit, the loss is yours. There is no going back. You need to use this deposit wisely so as to get from it the utmost in business success, health and happiness. Use it so as to get the most done.

The clock is running, and you need to make the most of your time. Think about the value of these units of time:

■ **The value of one year.** To recognize the value of a year, ask a student who failed to achieve the grade.

■ **The value of one month.** Ask a mother who gave birth to a premature baby.

■ **The value of one week.** Ask the person who edits the weekly newspaper.

■ **The value of one hour.** Ask the people sitting waiting for someone vital to join a meeting.

■ **The value of one minute.** Ask the person who just missed their train and so failed to make an important presentation.

■ **The value of one millisecond.** Ask the person who won the silver medal.

If you should have done something and you didn't, you can't have the time back! So learn to make the most of it.

Remember that time waits for no one.

1.2

Ask for clear instructions

Often people can be a bit vague when they are giving instructions or explaining what they want. This may not appear to be much of a problem at first, but it can lead to a lot of wasted time. If someone asks you to do something for them, make sure you are 100% certain about what's required.

1 Whenever possible, get a written instruction or request; the act of writing down instructions makes people think more carefully and fully about what they actually want. It also saves you having a difference of opinion later about what was said and heard.

2 Whether written or spoken, try to get the request in as much specific detail as possible. For instance, "Pick me up outside the west door of the HSBC Bank", rather than "Pick me up at the bank."

3 Getting it done late is no good; you need to know the deadline for the job to be done. Again, make sure you get specific detail: "by 5.30pm on Friday afternoon" rather than "by Friday" or "this week" or "as soon as possible".

one minute wonder Before you start on any task, make sure you know the What, Where, When and How of the job you are about to undertake. If you don't, you will quite possibly end up wasting all the time you spend.

At work there may be specific quality standards to be achieved. For example, your manager wants a report on sales to date this year, broken down by product and region and cross referenced by sales person. The report is needed by 5pm on Friday the 12th of July.

Ok, those were your instructions, which on the face of it seemed clear, with a specific deadline. However, is there really enough detail about how the report should be submitted? You shouldn't be starting on this task until you know the specific details, such as:

■ Is it in draft form or final form?
■ Is it to be in a specific format (for example a company template)?
■ Does it need to feed into other standard company forms?

If the person giving the instructions doesn't offer all the essential detail, then you are going to have to ask. Never be shy about asking for more detail. The best way to start is to repeat back your understanding of the instruction to the person who gave it to you. That's what pilots do!

See also Secret 7.3 when you need to *give* good instructions.

Getting it right first time is always better than having to come back and do it again.

1.3

See the relevance of the bigger picture

People often talk about the 'bigger picture', often meaning the strategy of the organization or overall purpose. You need to know how what you are doing is contributing to the 'bigger picture' and moving the organization closer to that final goal.

It is really easy to simply accept any instruction from your superiors as being 'right': not something to question, but something just to do, even if you can't see its relevance.

It isn't necessarily a criticism of your boss if you question an instruction; it may be simply that you want to understand how the instruction fits into the overall purpose of the organization. Understanding this increases your commitment to doing it and doing it well, whereas if you are doing something that, quite literally, has no point you will quickly become disillusioned. Likewise, it is valuable to recognize how doing something that doesn't benefit the organization is potentially valueless to them, therefore making you (or at least your job) unnecessary.

What is important is to ensure that you check the relevance to the bigger picture in a way that doesn't seem to be critical of your boss. Opposite are some tips on how to do this.

one minute wonder You may have to do a mix of tasks, some of which are relevant to the bigger picture and some of which are irrelevant. Make sure you know the level of importance to attach to the irrelevant ones.

1 Approach your boss in private, not in front of other people, when you want to check the relevance of the tasks requested of you.

2 Ask 'open' questions, which cannot be answered simply with a "Yes" or "No". Ask how, why, what, where and who questions rather that do/does, will, can. For example, "I need to understand how this contributes to the departmental sales activity" or "Where does this feed into the manufacturing process?"

3 If necessary 'sell' the benefits to the manager of taking the time to explain this: "I want to do this job really well for you, so can you explain…" or "If I understand the value of this task, I can ensure that it gets the priority it deserves…"

4 If the task isn't actually relevant to the bigger picture, but the boss still wants it done, ask what its priority is in relation to the tasks you have that are relevant.

5 Thank your boss for explaining it. You'll quickly 'train' your boss to ensure that you only get relevant tasks without asking!

Knowing how your tasks relate to the bigger picture helps both you and your boss to organize the workload.

1.4

Identify what's relevant to you

In work you need to be sure that the things you do are really part of your job (and that means your boss's view of your job). Similarly, outside work you want to be sure that doing things for others doesn't stop you doing things for yourself.

There are many reasons why people find themselves doing things at work that aren't their job. The same goes for non-work life; whether it is doing things for your family or the community. For example:

■ Their job is ill defined.
■ The person who complains the least gets the task.
■ This person will do it better than anyone else, either because they have the skill or the commitment.
■ The task is something that a person likes, so they volunteer to do it.

one minute wonder Consider the proverb: "The cobbler's children are the worst shod in town." This is a description of someone who has become confused about what's relevant to them personally.

■ When does it matter if you are doing something that isn't your job? If you are distracted into other activities that are not included in your formal targets, but which prevent you from achieving your targets, or stop you achieving them on time, then you have failed. Therefore, if you take on extra things, make sure that you really do have time for them and they are for a purpose that's relevant to you. For example, your boss is looking for a volunteer to do a departmental survey. Nobody else wants to take on this extra work, but you volunteer because you want to know more about how the department works and you want to network with people, not because you feel obliged.

■ When does it matter if you are distracted into doing things for others in your non-work life? Of course it is good to be altruistic and to help others. However, some people become so distracted by helping others that they leave no time to do the tasks that are important to them personally. For example, when you find you are spending far more time helping with the school committee than helping your own children with their homework, then you need to step back from the situation, identify your real priorities and arrange your time better. Also, if you take on extra things to help others, make sure this is not just because you are procrastinating on something else you ought to be doing for yourself, or using the other thing as an excuse. For example, have you agreed to decorate your brother's flat because you really want to help him, or because you are secretly putting off committing to that evening class you've been talking about for ages?

For more advice on this subject, see Chapter 5 on saying "no".

Remind yourself of what's really relevant in your workload.

1.5

Do the 'right' things right

The previous two Secrets in this book discuss doing what is 'relevant', but you also have to do what is 'right'. There are various levels of 'rightness' to judge things by: moral, ethical, legal and practical.

■ **Moral, ethical and legal.** Your personal morality and ethics will reflect the religious teachings and codes of law in your country. If you work for a global organization you may have to bear in mind differences between the moral and ethical norms in your native country and others you might come into contact with. Likewise, make sure that what you do is legally right under the laws of your organization, your country and any international laws affecting it. For example, few people would

case study An importer was making a margin of 4% on high-volume, low-cost, perishable stock. This did not feel 'right' in practical terms because it was a very low margin. Not only that, some of the importer's customers were asking for more environmentally friendly and ethically produced stock that would fulfil the 'right' values for them. The importer decided to

> **"Real integrity is doing the right thing, knowing that nobody's going to know whether you did it or not" Oprah Winfrey, American TV personality**

consider that it would be doing the 'right' thing to sell alcohol-related products in a country that bans alcohol. That may be an extreme example, but the point is that to keep up your motivation, it's essential that you do the things that feel 'right' according to your moral code, and to do them 'right' – or 100% correctly to the best of your abilities.

■ **Practical.** There is a phrase in English: 'busy fools'. This is used to describe people who are always busy and active but are doing the 'wrong' things. The 'wrong' things could be:

- ■ Things which aren't relevant (see Secrets 1.3 and 1.4).
- ■ Things which your customer doesn't want, need or value (see Secret 4.4).
- ■ Things which are of lesser value.

Make sure that the things you do are 'right' in every sense of the word.

introduce another line of products that were less perishable and lighter to transport, and which sold for a 15% margin. By doing the 'right' thing, the importer was able to continue to provide the original stock to the loyal customers while also increasing the product range and customer base, and protecting and expanding the business.

1.6

Plan for output, not activity

This piece of advice may seem obvious: we are looking at the subject of 'Getting Things Done' so of course we are going to plan for output (i.e. the end result) rather than the activity, aren't we? And yet, in the real world we often plan things the other way round – for activity rather than output.

Part of this mixed up focus comes from our schooling or our parents and the way we were treated as children. "Oh yes, he practises his piano for an hour every day" is an example of the measurement of activity rather than output. Similarly, "We set half an hour of homework each day", or "You will spend three years at university".

All these approaches measure activity rather than output. Indeed, the output is expected to happen almost by chance. "If you spend an hour hitting piano keys each day you are bound to play a good tune eventually." This encourages the child to become a 'clock-watcher': "When I've been hitting piano keys for an hour I can go and play." The child then concentrates on the minute hand rather than focusing on the piano playing.

This behaviour tends to be carried on in our work life; we measure things by how long we are doing something rather than aiming to achieve a specific outcome in the available time. Of course, this is reinforced by the fact that we are often paid a salary of X per year, or Y per month, or Z per hour. Evidentally, it's payment for the passage of time, not output!

So when you are setting yourself goals (or deciding what to do today) aim for the Outcome not the Activity.

Outcome rather than...	Activity
Buy essential groceries	Go shopping
Drain pond	Dig ditch
Solve customer complaints	Answer 25 phone calls per hour
Iron 25 shirts	Spend four hours ironing
Build a house	Be on site for a month
Find answers	Do research

With many tasks you will need to break them down into smaller outcomes in order to make them more visible.

Big outcome becomes...	More visible outcomes
Build a house	Complete foundations
	Build walls to ceiling level
	Construct weatherproof roof

This will help you to focus on getting things done, which will add a sense of urgency, allow you to measure your success and generally improve your morale as well.

It is very satisfying to see that you have achieved something, rather than just spending time doing something.

1.7

DREAM to get more done

You'll often hear people say that they wish they had more hours in the day, or that they dream of having more time. Well now they can at least use the mnemonic DREAM to help them achieve more in the time they have....

DREAM is a simple five-option way to manage the things that come into your in-tray during the working day – or the requests you get from your spouse/boss/customers/or staff.

When you receive a request for help or an instruction, decide immediately on one of these five courses of actions. Don't ignore it or put off dealing with the issue.

1 **Delegate it.** If it is appropriate to do so, you should delegate it to either a peer or a subordinate. Delegating a job requires you to ensure that the person to whom you delegate has the skill, the time, the authority and the responsibility for completing the job to the proper standard and deadline. If you don't ensure that they have all of these things, then you haven't 'delegated', you have 'dumped'! (See Secret 7.4.)

"One thing is sure. We have to do something. We have to do the best we know how at the moment... If it doesn't turn out right, we can modify it as we go along.**"**

Franklin D. Roosevelt (1882–1945), US President

2 **Reflect or refuse it.** If appropriate you should refuse to undertake this task on the grounds that it isn't right for you to be doing it or reflect it away to the appropriate person, even if that person is the source of the request!

3 **Escalate it.** You can pass it straight up to your boss if it is something that ultimately she or he will need to deal with.

4 **Action it.** Get it done immediately if it is definitely your responsibility. Avoid simply adding it to your in-tray – action it immediately, whilst the source of the request waits if possible!

5 **Make a time for it.** If it is definitely your responsibility and you can't do it immediately (either because of other priorities or reasons), schedule a time to do it. Either insert it into your prioritized 'to do' list (see Secret 1.10) or set a time in your diary to deal with it.

Consciously think 'DREAM' with each item in your in-tray and each request, then decide how to manage it.

1.8

Have a personal vision or mission

You don't want your career to stand still; you want to be sure that what you do is relevant to moving you towards your longer term career goals. There are two elements you need to have in mind here.

What are your long-term career goals?

Most of us are simply grateful to have a decent job and a wage packet at the end of each week or month, but we also need to have a vision of where we want to be in the future. You may want to carve out a long-term career with your current employer or you may want to set up your own business in the future, but the most important thing is to know what you want out of life.

Visualize yourself at the age 50 or 60 years.

- How respected are you?
- Where do you live and work?
- What kind of family life do you have?
- What do you do for fun?

"If you don't know where you are going, any road will get you there" Lewis Carroll, English author

Deciding the answers to these questions will help you to define the type of job you work in today and next year in order to get to where you want to be. Many people find it really helpful to write out their vision, either like an essay or a series of bullet points.

What medium-term actions are relevant to achieving your long-term career goals?

You now have to ensure that everything you do is relevant to you in your current and next job. Especially if you are working at a junior level, assess each instruction to ensure that it is within the job description of your current job. You are assessed against your job description, so doing things that aren't covered in your job description is like spending time asleep, unless... a task is clearly proving your ability to be promoted to the next job up! If you are working at a more senior level, ask yourself if you are getting all the right things done, or could you be prioritizing or delegating more efficiently? Are you genuinely working each day to achieve your long-term career goals?

Look at Secret 1.4 as well since it looks in more depth at the short-term aspect of your current job.

Write down your long-term career goals and what you need to do in the medium term to achieve them.

1.9

Know WIIFM

The mnemonic WIIFM stands for What's In It For Me? It may sound selfish, but in terms of getting things done, WIIFM is important because it can provide you with a motivation to want to do something, as opposed to doing something simply because you think you have to do it.

It may seem odd to be talking about having to find out "what's in it for me", but the reality is that every job has its good bits and its bad bits: things that we like doing and things that we hate doing. Usually the WIIFM good bits of a job are fairly easy to find:

- I enjoy it.
- I find it easy.
- It makes me look good/feel good.
- It moves me closer to promotion.

one minute wonder WIIFMS are very rarely about financial reward, so think outside the money-box!

"Work spares us from three evils: boredom, vice and need" Voltaire, French Enlightenment writer

Finding the WIIFM factor in the bad bits of the job is often more difficult. However, if we can identify the WIIFM it helps motivate us to do the bad bits properly and quickly.

You may find the WIIFM in one of two areas of the bad bits of your job.

Positive WIIFMs such as:

- I don't enjoy it but it makes me look good.
- I don't enjoy it but it brings me closer to promotion.
- I'm not very good at it but by doing it I get better.

Nastiness avoidance WIIFMS such as:

- Once I've done it, it is out of the way for another month/quarter/year.
- If I can get it done the boss will stop hassling me to do it.
- As soon as it is out of the way I can stop worrying about it.
- If I do this then I'm safe from the authorities/criticism.

If you can find the "what's in it for me?" factor you can motivate yourself to do almost anything.

1.10

Make 'to do' lists

Some people love 'to do' lists and others hate them! What cannot be denied is that 'to do' lists help you to remember what it is that you need to do, and the more tasks you have to do, the more valuable the list.

■ **List all tasks.** List the one-off things as well as listing any everyday, weekly or monthly tasks.

■ **Break down the tasks.** Write as much detail as you can. This gives you a better chance of accurately estimating the time each task will take. For example, if you have to move to another workstation, break it down into the individual tasks:

■ Pack boxes
■ Disconnect pc & phone
■ Move desk
■ Move chair and filing cabinet
■ Move pc & phone

one minute wonder Many software programs and even mobile phones nowadays have a 'to do' list function (sometimes called a 'task' list). These are generally nothing more sophisticated than the type of paper list recommended here.

"Organizing is what you do before you do something, so that when you do it, it's not all mixed up"

A.A. Milne, English author of 'Winnie-the-Pooh'

■ **Look at your list at the beginning of each day.** Remind yourself of all the things you need to get done.

■ **Approach the tasks methodically.** Start working your way through the list in a logical order (see Secrets 3.1 to 3.5).

■ **Periodically check your list through the day.** Tick off or cross out the individual items on the list as you complete them.

■ **Keep the list highly visible.** Not only do you need it to hand to remind yourself of the different things that still need to be done but you can also show the list to anyone who comes to you with a new task; this is evidence of your workload!

■ **Update your list daily.** Last thing each day, sit quietly for ten minutes and write a list of all the things you have to do the next day. Remember that something carried over is probably now more urgent than it was before.

■ **File your lists.** You daily lists are a record of when you did things. Lots of people write the list in their desk diary or in a notebook; this keeps the lists in date order, which is handy when you need to check back to see when you did something.

The bluntest of pencils is better than the sharpest of minds. Write it down so that you won't forget it!

Knowing how to do things

Once you know what to do you need to work out some of the 'hows'. If you are working in a large organization it is important to know how to fit in by doing things in a certain way that fits into a bigger process. If you don't do this then you will end up with as bad an outcome as if you did nothing! You also need to know how you will be measured, which will enable you to measure your own ability to get things done.

2.1

Decide if 'how' is important

Once you know what you have to do, your next challenge is working out how you are going to do it. In some cases this will be entirely your choice but in others there will be restrictions that prevent certain methods, or prescribe a single 'right' way to complete the task.

A task that is a pure 'one-off', a never-to-be-repeated thing, can probably be done anyway you want so long as you do it in a way that is legal and ethical (see Secret 1.5). However, if a task is something that has been done before or will need to be done again, then you will have to be more thoughtful about the bigger picture.

■ **Approaching a task that has been done before.** In this instance you face a little challenge. You want to make sure that you aren't 're-inventing the wheel'; struggling to find a way to complete the task when someone else has already found a way that is quick, simple and effective. However, you also want to make sure that the task isn't being done in an inefficient way simply because everyone assumes that the way it was done before was best (see Secret 2.3).

"T'aint what you do, it's the way that you do it, that's what gets results" **Sy Oliver and Trummy Young, jazz singers**

■ **Approaching a task that will be repeated in the future.** Here you have two challenges. Firstly, you need to ensure that you record how you do the task so that you can easily do it again the same way, or so that you can pass the instructions to somebody else if they are going to have to do it next time. This also allows you to see how you could improve on the method you used. Secondly, you need to complete the task in a way that is repeatable, for example by not using up all the resources available.

■ **Approaching a task that is part of a larger task, perhaps company wide.** The most important element here is to know at what point and in what state the task arrives with you and the same information for you to pass it on to the next person in the overall process. This is important because it dictates your start and finish times, place and the quality standard you can expect of your raw materials, and that your successor can expect from you. (See also Secret 2.2.)

Find out if a task has been done before, or if it has to be repeated or if it relates to a larger task, before you decide exactly how you are going to do it.

2.2

Fit into a bigger process

If the thing you are trying to do is part of a bigger process, then you are going to have to consider that factor before you start on the task. The bigger process could be solely yours or it could be department- or company-wide.

To take a basic example that anyone can relate to, let's look at the bigger process of providing tea and coffee for a group of 45 people at work. Imagine that your part of the task is to make the individual teas and coffees, while other people take the orders, deliver the drinks, etc.

The overall process may look like this:

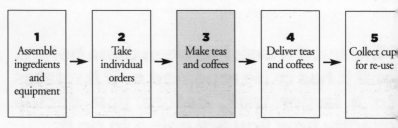

(Your task is shaded)

In order for you to fit into the bigger process you need to know, in advance, whether step 1 has been done properly. You will also need to know whether step 2 creates:

■ An expectation that individual cups will arrive with milk and sugar already in the beverage, or on the saucer in sachets, or on a common use basket on the tray.
■ An expectation that the refreshments will be delivered at a specific time.

(And if the orders in step 2 are written down, can you read the writing?)

In order to complete your task and allow someone else to fulfil step 4 you will need to know whether you actually need to put the 45 cups onto trays as the last part of your task or whether that is the first part of someone else's task.

You will also see that step 5 feeds into step 1 so that the process can be repeated. This is particularly important if the tasks are to be done by someone else next time – for example, if you operate a 'rota-system'.

Making the tea and coffee may not actually be part of your job, but this principle of fitting into a bigger process extends to manufacturing, building, customer-service, banking and pretty much any job in any industry. It is a fundamental of teamwork to ensure that all the individuals involved in the bigger process are aiming towards the same end result: in this instance 45 people all getting a nice cup of tea or coffee, when and where they need it!

Fitting into a bigger process means understanding the full process, then all working together to deliver success.

2.3

Find out how others do it

It is always worth investigating how others may have done a task in the past. Then compare it with your task and use your judgement to decide whether to follow a tried and trusted method or to develop a new, better way. Ask the questions listed here.

■ Has anyone in this company ever done this before? (Whether in the company or for a previous employer.) If not…

case study Robert, a manager, was tasked with purchasing a fleet of small cars for use by a pipelining crew in North Africa. His bosses suggested that he look at the vehicles used by a partner organization based in France. This organization used Renault 4 hatchbacks as they were robust, economical, readily available and easy to maintain. Robert was dubious, though, because the environment of the Libyan Desert was

Does any other company in my country do something similar? If not…

Does any other company globally do something similar?

If you find someone who already does this, how do they do it?

What similarities are there between the country in which they do it and this country? Are the Political, Economic, Social, Technical, Legal and Environmental (PESTLE) factors similar or the same?

What differences are there? (PESTLE again.)

Would their method work here?

If we think it would work, shall we copy it? Or do we need to make some changes to their method in order to make it work?

Think about the similarities, differences and 'PESTLE' factors when comparing tasks.

very different to France (he was considering the E of the PESTLE factors). He had one car shipped to his base in the Desert as a trial. After three days all the windows fell out due to the extreme heat expansion of the car's bodywork in the desert – not a problem encountered in France. Robert and his bosses were relieved that he hadn't leased a whole fleet of them based on simply copying the partner organization.

2.4

Set quality measures

When you do something you want to be sure that it is done 'right' – not 'nearly right' or 'almost right' or even 'just about right'. The only way to be certain that we will recognize 'right' when we have achieved it is to set quality measures.

If you look at any well-known quality measures (ISO 9001 for example), you will see that the concept of 'quality' is simply a measurable standard that an organization *says* it will achieve and then achieves. (It is not – as some believe – an international standard of attainment that compares one nation's, or company's, production with another.)

You can and should set quality measures for yourself in your personal life as well as work life. Consider factors like these:

■ **Your skill level in the subject area.** If you are new to something you may well set a lower target to begin with than you would wish to achieve in the future. For example, if your personal ambition is to run a five-minute mile, but you have never run a mile before in your life you won't achieve it on your first attempts. Maybe you could start with an eight-minute mile as a quality measure.

■ **The amount of time you can invest in getting to the outcome.** For example, if you want to pack an overnight bag but you only have

"Quality is never an accident; it is always the result of intelligent effort" John Ruskin, 19th-century art critic

a short time before your train leaves, you won't aim to fold every garment neatly. Your measure of quality will perhaps be to get to your destination with all you need, albeit with slightly crumpled clothing.

The value of the outcome to you or your organization. For example, if the task concerned is business critical, you will set higher targets than if the task is relatively unimportant. This works for 'positive-business-critical' tasks, such as structuring a major deal that will contribute 40% of company income, and 'negative-business-critical' tasks, such as complying with an international law, for which the penalty for breaking is a fine of millions of dollars.

The tolerances of other things if this task is part of a larger process. For example, if the task is weighing freight for air transport purposes it may be very important to have an accurate standard, since the inability to know exactly what weight the cargo is will seriously affect the fuel consumption and range of the aircraft.

Just measuring output in an empirical way improves the level of output: this is known as the 'Hawthorne Effect'. The project was carried out between 1924 and 1927 at the Hawthorne Works in Chicago, which assembled telephone equipment. It was discovered that the very act of observing and measuring the output of the group of workers increased the levels of output in comparison to periods when they were not observed or measured.

Setting quality measures improves the standard and level of output.

2.5

Know how to KISS

KISS is another mnemonic; in this instance it stand
for Keep It Short and Simple! It may be tempting to
try to find a state-of-the-art, technically clever way
to do something, but there are some real issues tha
crop up when you do anything in a more compli-
cated way than is absolutely necessary.

No matter what you are trying to do there is always a range o
short, simple ways of doing it and a range of slower, more comple
ways. Unless you really need to come up with a technically advance
product or method, then the quick and simple solution is usually the bes
Here are two case studies that have been annotated with th
present and longer term advantages and disadvantages of the short and
simple 'KISS' method.

case study 1

Early car makers wanted to put a windscreen washer spray on their cars
They decided that, rather than design a pump system and provid
power, they would simply connect the valve of the spare tyre to a seale
water bottle and use the pressure to force the water over the windscreen

Advantages to manufacturer	Disadvantages to manufacturer
Reduced development or testing costs Reduced manufacturing costs Quicker move to market Less risk of failure/warranty claim	None

Advantages to customer	Disadvantages to customer
Cheaper to buy Less owner maintenance Cheaper replacement cost	Potentially flat spare when needed to replace a tyre. However, the car carried a foot pump, so not a serious disadvantage

case study 2

Tasked with reducing in-flight catering costs, an airline looked at various options. Finally someone suggested simply removing a single olive from all the salad options on the menus. This action saved $40,000 in a single year.

Advantages	Disadvantages
$40,000 saving No new equipment Simple process change Easy to check Easy to change	None (it is such an insignificant change to the customer that it is unlikely to be noticed)

If you have a choice between a simple and complex way to do something, always go for the simple way.

Knowing when to do things

The secrets of prioritizing are covered in this chapter. You will learn how to assess the cost/benefit ratios of individual tasks and how to create a logical sequence for doing things. We explain the 'quick win' approach and how you can identify your most productive time of day. The chapter also shows how you can get things done whilst you are waiting for other things to happen.

3.1

Prioritize this – or that?

You often hear people say that they haven't done something because they "haven't had the time". Generally what they mean is that it wasn't high enough on their list of priorities to get done in the time available. This is fine as long as they have actually set sensible priorities rather than tackling things in a random or illogical order.

If you have a 'to do' list (Secret 1.10) – which is a very good way of ensuring you don't forget things – you can make use of it to work out a sensible order for your tasks by making 'paired comparisons'.

Let's assume you have six things to do on your list. For the purposes of this explanation, we will simply refer to them as a, b, c, d, e and f. Compare each one against each of the others in turn to assess which of each pair is the more *urgent*. Then do the same to assess which of the pair is the more *important*.

On the next page is a table to show the decisions made. The sections with grey shading show 'Importance' whilst the clear sections show 'Urgency'. So, if you were to compare tasks a and b, for example, you would see that b is the more important task, while a is the more urgent. And if you were to compare b and c, you would see that c is both more important and more urgent.

Task	a	b	c	d	e	f
a		b	c	d	a	f
b	a		c	d	e	f
c	a	c		c	c	c
d	d	b	d		d	f
e	a	e	c	d		e
f	a	b	c	f	f	

Once you have drawn up a table, as above, add up the number of times that each task was judged the more "urgent":

a=4 b=2 c=3 d=3 e=1 f=2

So, in terms of urgency, the order for things to be done is a, c and d, b and f, then e. However, you also need to take into account the importance of each task, so count the number of times each was judged the more "important":

a=1 b=1 c=5 d=3 e=2 f=3

So, in terms of importance, the order for things to be done is c, d and f, e, then a and b. This shows that a is very urgent but not very important. If you can do it quickly, you should do it; if not, you'll need to find a way to accommodate task a while still allowing you to do the important tasks. You might delegate it, for example, or try to get permission to leave it until a later time.

Set your priorities to ensure that you get done what needs to be done.

3.2

Look at effort versus pay-off

"Stop messing about and do something worthwhile!" If you have ever been on the receiving end of a comment like this you will understand the value of this next way of deciding what your priorities are. This method looks at each task on the basis of effort versus pay-off.

This is a bit like a mini 'cost/benefit' analysis, so you must have a pretty good idea, before you start, of how difficult or expensive the task will be to fulfil and also what value you are going to get out of the task at the end.

1 To do this you start by judging a task in terms of its difficulty or cost. You can do this on a numerical scale (of comparable cost such as man-hours or dollars) or on a more subjective scale perhaps ranging from 'easy' to 'very difficult' or 'almost free' to 'very expensive'.

2 Then you judge the task according to the pay-off or value you expect to come from this task. Again you can be empirical (e.g. man-hours saving or revenue generated), or you can be more wide-ranging, such as 'little intrinsic value' up to 'worth its weight in gold'.

3 Once you have assessed each task in both ways you can plot them on a 'graph', as below, to compare their relative merits.

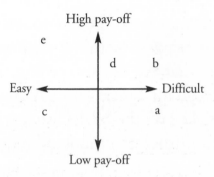

This suggests that we should do the tasks in the following order:

1 e because this is high pay-off for little effort.
2 d because it is a fairly high pay-off and easier than b.
3 c because it is very easy compared with b.
4 b because the pay-off is much higher than a.
5 a because it is the hardest task with no better pay-off than c.

By assessing the ratio of effort to pay-off, you ensure that you are doing things that are worthwhile.

3.3

Go for quick wins

As human beings we really like to feel that we are actually achieving something; that we are going somewhere; that we are succeeding. This is why people often go for 'quick wins'. A quick win is the first thing ticked off the 'to do' list; it is the first step taken in the journey of a thousand miles.

A 'quick win' is a result we can achieve with minimal effort or within a short period of time. The length of the short period of time will be relative to the nature of your activity. 'Quick wins' are important whether you are working on something alone or as part of a team or as part of a longer process or project.

■ When working alone, a 'quick win' is a personal motivator. You get to tick something off the 'to do' list, which means you have a little less left to do and something to say you have finished.
■ When working as a team, the 'quick win' is something for the team to know about that starts to create a feeling of belonging to the team. It is something 'we' have achieved (even if only one person actually did it!) as it moves us towards our shared goal.

"A journey of a thousand miles begins with a single step" Lao Tzu

When working as part of a larger or longer process or project, it is something for people to be told about that reassures them that all is moving forward and that they will be in action soon.

A 'quick win' can also be very beneficial to demonstrate progress to higher management or a customer/stakeholder base when you are engaged in a longer process or project, especially when there is expected to be delay and frustration.

Ways in which you can achieve a 'quick win':

Defining the objective of a task may be a 'quick win' if the task itself is quite complex.

Similarly, the production of a detailed plan is itself a 'quick win', which helps you feel as if you are getting somewhere.

Fulfilling something on the left-hand side of the diagram in Secret 3.2 will make you feel as though you are getting through the 'to do' list.

The act of forming the team can be a 'quick win' in big projects or complex processes involving many people.

'Quick wins' are almost always valid, so publicize and celebrate them.

3.4

Use your body clock

Are you a 'morning person'? Does your energy star
to tail off in mid-afternoon? Or are you a 'night owl'
who is full of spark and get-up-and-go at midnight
Not all of us are the same, and one of the best way
to get things done is to identify when your body i
best suited to fulfilling different tasks.

■ **The body clock.** The proper term is 'circadian biorhythm' (*circadia*
in Latin literally means 'throughout the day'). Your circadian biorhythm
is controlled by around 100,000 cells around the hypothalamus in th
brain. These cells control the release of different chemicals that hav
different effects. For example, at around 7am most people have lov
levels of serotonin; this tends to make people grumpy! At around 4pn
adrenaline levels are generally highest so physical activity or jobs tha
require good hand-eye co-ordination are more likely to be successful. A
7pm melatonin is released in preparation for sleep, so most of us ar
fairly drowsy at this time of day.

■ **Working at night.** The body clock is tuned to daylight, so if you ar
someone who works shifts you can help yourself to retune your bod
clock by ensuring that you sleep in the dark. If you fail to do this you

may find that you have a lot of difficulties since, for example, blood is at its thickest generally between 2am and 6am, reducing energy levels and reaction times.

Typical body clocks. Body clocks are also different for people of different ages: the times mentioned before apply to many infants, children and adults, whereas many teenagers' body clocks are set two to three hours later than other people.

Understanding your own body clock. Keep a diary of your levels of energy and motivation, adeptness and success. You will start to see patterns emerging. You can then use these patterns to help you to schedule tasks into your day to make best use of your most appropriate biorhythms. For example, I know that I am best at doing little domestic-type chores early in the day; late morning I'm good at research and writing; early afternoon I'm best at something a bit more physical; and later in the afternoon I'm back to the research and writing.

Understand your personal biorhythm patterns, then schedule tasks to make best use of them.

3.5

Schedule your tasks

Sometimes you will have a number of subtasks to fulfil in order to complete a bigger, composite job. On such occasions a simple 'to do' list isn't enough because jobs have to be done in a very specific order. Scheduling makes sure that you 'ready, aim, fire' rather than 'fire, ready, aim'.

■ Schedules. A schedule is a 'to do' list of tasks that are inter-related. For instance, if you are managing an office move for 30 people, the individual tasks need to be carried out in a specific order: you can't move the desks until the PCs have been disconnected and moved, and you can't set up the PCs in the new offices until there are desks to put them on. So for a bigger job, you need to schedule the individual tasks.

■ Dependencies. When scheduling you will need to put the tasks in order according to 'dependencies': these are covered in detail in Secrets 3.7, 3.8 and 3.9.

■ Types of schedule. A schedule can be a simple numerical list with the tasks shown in order of priority, or it can take a more diagrammatic form. Opposite are two commonly used examples, showing a straightforward sequence of tasks.

Pert chart

Each task appears in the sequence in which it must be done. The advantage of a Pert chart is its clarity and simplicity. This is a Pert chart showing the sequence of building a simple structure.

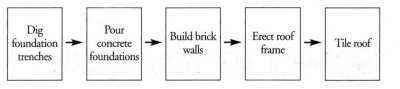

Gantt chart

Again each task appears in the sequence in which it must be done, but here both the date when it is scheduled and the amount of time it is expected to take (plus leeway on the first Wednesday and second Monday) are also shown.

	Mon	Tue	Wed	Thur	Fri	Mon	Tue	Wed	Thur
Dig foundation trenches	▓								
Pour concrete foundations		▓							
Build brick walls				▓					
Erect roof frame								▓	
Tile roof								▓	▓

Effective scheduling will save you and others time.

3.6

Schedule for task dependency

Have you ever tried to do something and found that you can't start on it immediately because it depends on doing some other task first. If you have, then you know what 'task dependency' is. By scheduling for task dependency, you avoid having to backtrack.

Task dependency is defined as the relationship between two tasks, in which the ability to start or finish a task depends upon the starting or finishing of another task.

For example, you start to move your desk into another office (a 10-minute job) but discover that you can't move the desk because the drawers are full of files. You go to take out the files (a five-minute job) but you then realize that you haven't got anything to put the files in to

case study A company was planning to set up a new factory in a new location. They didn't consider the possibility of dependency between constructing the factory building and buying the manufacturing

eep them in order. Now you have a choice: go and find a box (a 30-minute job) or let the files become mixed up and spend time re-sorting hem in the new office (also a 30-minute job).

Think through the sequence. In Secret 1.10 we learned to break own tasks on the 'to do' list into the most detail possible. If we do this, much of the task dependency will become obvious. As in the example with the desk move, the sequential nature of the job is fairly clear. ometimes, however, we won't have anticipated the dependency etween tasks (see case study below).

Scheduling for more people. Task dependency is a common tool n project management, where you'll be scheduling for a number of eople. Here, sequences can overlap and you might have two depend-nt tasks going on at the same time. For example, one person could be nstalling a computer network and, whilst that is still part done, another erson can be setting up the individual PCs.

Scheduling for task dependency saves you having to stop and go back.

machinery to go in it. They built the building first, then ound they couldn't get machinery in through the door! Had they identified and ordered the machinery irst, they could have built the doors big enough.

3.7

Schedule for resource dependency

In an ideal world we'd all have all the equipment and material that we wanted for every task. Sadly we don't live in that ideal world; we live in a world where money, machinery, material and manpower are all limited. This means that we have to schedule with a consideration to the availability of resources.

To schedule for resource dependencies you must consider when you need things in order to complete the task. You can cover all the resource scheduling requirements following the mnemonic TIME! (The '!' is significant.)

■ **Time.** Make sure that you will have a suitable chunk of time available as a resource. For example, there isn't much point scheduling to start a three-hour task 30 minutes before your day or shift ends.

Input from others. You need to schedule around the provision of input from others, whether it is a colleague providing information, a customer being there to buy, or a manager authorizing something.

Material. Whether you are going to have all the materials available before you start or whether you are going to operate on a 'Just-In-Time' basis, you must remember to schedule the common consumables as well. If you are producing reports, remember not just the printed covers and spiral binders but also the paper and the ink. If you are making concrete you need the cement, sand and aggregate, but don't forget the petrol and oil for the concrete mixer, and even the water!

Equipment. If you have to share equipment such as printers, lathes or cars you must ensure that you have booked them for the time you schedule. That will probably mean checking availability before you write your schedule. If equipment has to be hired in you will need to also factor in delivery and checking.

! It is said that a last-minute job never lasts a minute. If you schedule a task to be completed just as the deadline for its delivery appears, then something will go wrong. (If you don't believe this, think of how many times your plans have gone wrong because someone upon whom you were relying couldn't get their bit done in time because they left it to the last minute.) Schedule things to be finished well before they need to be delivered.

You can't complete a task without the resources, so plan your schedule around having them.

3.8

Schedule for concurrent activity

When you look at any schedule there are always periods of time when you have to wait for something else to finish or happen. When you are working out a schedule you can deliberately plan for 'concurrent activity'.

Concurrent activity is an activity being undertaken whilst something else is going on. Examples of periods when concurrent activity is appropriate might include:

- Waiting for the kettle to boil when you are making tea.
- Waiting for paint to dry when you are decorating.
- Waiting for concrete or mortar to set when you are building.
- Waiting for the printer to print all the copies when you are creating documents.
- Waiting for a colleague to add their part to a report you have started.
- Waiting for your boss to check (or sign off) something you have done to date, so you can carry on with the rest of the task.
- Waiting for permission from authorities for something such as planning permission.

You should plan to use this time constructively to complete other tasks that can be fitted in effectively. For example:

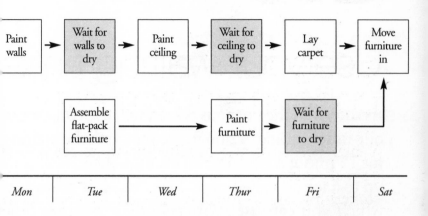

Planning to use time in this way allows you to get a lot more done in a shorter period, whether in your home life or in your work life. If you commute to work by train and you travel for 30 minutes each way each day, that is 10 hours per week, over a year that means you are 'waiting' to get to work for 62 working days. I studied for my professional exams whilst travelling to work each day.

Scheduling for concurrent activity can get a job done in half the time that it would otherwise take.

3.9

Use your waiting time

As shown in the previous Secret, we all spend a lot of our time waiting. Though we may only be waiting for 15 minutes here and 20 minutes there, it all adds up to a lot of wasted time. Here are ideas of ways in which you can use short periods of waiting time more productively.

We might be waiting for our boss to tell us what to do or to sign off what we have done, waiting for a colleague to finish something so we can do our bit, or waiting for something to happen, such as an email to arrive or paint to dry. If we know that we are going to have these little breaks during the day when we are going to be waiting, then we can see whether some of the jobs on the 'to do list could be broken up into smaller chunks and used to fill these waiting times.

1 The following are common tasks that can be slotted into little waiting times during the day:
■ Any form of writing, such as reports, letters, journals.
■ Making a quick phone call (e.g. to book a meeting room).
■ Asking someone a quick question or giving a quick answer.
■ Filing (electronic or manual).

- Clearing your in-tray.
- Reading through the manual for a piece of equipment.
- Reading a periodical, report or trade paper.
- Researching something on the Internet.
- Proofreading.
- Catching up on your expenses/balancing your chequebook.
- Grazing, power-napping or taking isometric exercise.
- Checking and updating your 'to do' list!

2 Person-specific tasks that can be slotted into any waiting times will fall into two categories: those you have to be at your desk/workstation for, and those that you can do anywhere. Which category a task falls into will depend on your job and whether you have a mobile phone, mobile Internet access etc. Only you can decide, but the trick is to plan.

Plan to use every minute of the working day, even those minutes when someone else keeps you waiting.

Working to your plan

A Scottish poet once said that no matter how carefully you plan, something always goes wrong! This chapter aims to help you identify and manage the things that go wrong and stop you from getting things done according to your plan. You will learn how to deal with distractions and how to minimize fatigue. It also suggests ways to make your workplace more efficient and ways to overcome your own inertia.

Deal with people distractions

You've written a 'to do' list. You've assured that all the things on the list are 'right'. You've prioritized your tasks. You've found simple and straightforward ways to do things. Then someone distracts you and all your plans are put to one side; you reach the end of the day with only half of them done. You must deal with distractions.

■ **Dealing with customers.** Customers can distract you whether you have a customer-facing role or work in the back office. If your primary function is to deal with customers then you simply have to accept this distraction and be as speedy and businesslike as you can. If you are not supposed to be customer-facing, then you need to direct the customer assertively to whoever should and can help them. (See also Secret 5.1.)

one minute wonder if you are a manager you will find that your staff are a huge source of distraction as they come to you for authority or advice, to lobby your support, lodge complaints or just be sociable! Use the DREAM method in Secret 1.7.

■ **Dealing with your boss.** You may find that your boss distracts you either with more tasks, advice or general discussion. Here a good 'to do' list becomes invaluable – it is evidence of how many tasks you already have to do and proof that you need to be given the space and time to do them. (See also Secret 5.1.)

■ **Dealing with colleagues/peers and staff.** Other people you work with may come to you for advice or support to discuss other aspects of work or purely socially. Here you will simply have to be assertive. You can use the methods described in Secrets 5.1 and 5.2, 7.2 or 7.4.

■ **Dealing with salespeople.** Depending on your position (at work; everyone is a sales target at home!) you may find that salespeople, in person or on the phone or by email are a distraction. Here you will again have to be assertive; if you want to discuss something with this salesperson you can use Secret 1.7 or the method in Secret 5.1. If you have no interest then you can use the methods in Secret 5.2.

Learn to deal with people distractions; it is a major key to getting things done.

4.2

Deal with other distractions

There are several other types of distraction that create problems. Obviously there are 'real' distractions: fire alarms, bomb warnings and disasters (man-made and natural). But far more disruptive than these are the entirely self-made distractions: going for a smoke, day-dreaming, gossiping, going for a coffee/tea, surfing the Internet, and generally getting side-tracked from the job in hand.

■ **Real distractions.** The only real distractions you should ever allow yourself are emergencies such as fire, hurricane, flood, etc. Even during a fire-alarm drill, you could probably utilize the time spent waiting at the drill point to do something (see Secret 3.9). Minor disturbances – such as the sound of someone hammering on the other side of the wall, or a group of people talking loudly nearby – while annoying, shouldn't be used as an excuse for serious distraction either.

one minute wonder Think like a laboratory rat! Lab rats used for behavioural studies are only given treats when they perform to standard. Only allow yourself your 'distraction treat' – that cigarette, coffee, tea, chat, surf etc – AFTER you have achieved a certain amount of things on your 'to do' list.

■ **Self-made distractions.** If you are prone to daydreaming, gossiping or surfing the Internet, then you need to recognize that fact and change your habits. You may not be able to stop completely (you may have created a reputation for being chatty with others that you cannot easily break, for example), but you need to learn to limit these activities to a time and a duration that is appropriate. Only gossip at formal breaks. Limit your Internet surfing to home time in the evenings. Most employers have rules about web-surfing that outlaw it at work anyway. Curtail your daydreaming to lunchtime or on your journey to work (assuming that you aren't driving!). Be disciplined with yourself.

■ **Getting side-tracked.** This is sometimes known jokingly as 'but-first syndrome'; as in "I'll do the stock take, but first I'll just tidy up all the products on the shelves". The stock take would take 30 minutes but tidying the shelves first will take an hour before you even start on the stock take. Having a visible 'to do' list and crossing off the completed tasks helps you to avoid 'but-first syndrome', although you still need to discipline yourself against it.

Discipline yourself against self-made distractions.

4.3

Use technology

What sets humans apart from other animals is our ability to use tools. Modern technology is simply the advanced versions of stone axes, wax tablets, quill pens and abacuses. However, whereas you could look at an axe and quickly work out how to use it, the same can't be said for a lot of technological tools! Here are some technology secrets that might actually help you get things done.

Modern technology advances at an amazing rate and we are all constantly under pressure to get on with doing things. The downside of this is that we often don't know the capability of the technology available. Humans invented tools to make jobs easier and quicker, so respect those who have gone before and ensure you don't re-invent the wheel.

■ **Desk phones.** Most desk phones have all sorts of capabilities that could unlock lots of time. Speed dial saves you from wasting time entering an 8- or 10-digit number; you just press one number. Phone memory saves you from wasting time looking up numbers. Redirect saves you from running round the office answering the phones of people who have gone into a meeting.

■ **Mobile phones/cellphones.** Your cellphone probably has predictive text to save you wasting time typing each letter of an SMS message. It also probably has the capacity to store common template messages, and to send messages to groups of people at a time.

■ **Computers.** Your PC probably has the capability to switch between screen displays, saving you from wasting time printing off a hard copy to refer to whilst you write a new document. It probably also allows you to create shortcuts on the desktop to documents you use frequently to save you wasting time going through scores of directories and files to find them. Look through your applications and menus, and you might be surprised at what you find.

It is estimated that around 40% of the capacity of software and hardware is not used because people don't know it is there. Use those periods of time when you are waiting for something else to read through those manuals – you might learn something within a few minutes that saves cumulative hours of time later!

Learn about the shortcuts and time-saving features of the technological tools that surround you.

4.4

Beware the Seven Wastes of Time

The so-called 'Lean' principles – applied in many manufacturing industries – identify about seven wastes in a typical business environment. Over the years I have developed this idea for the main wastes of time as well. Look through the Seven Wastes listed below and see how many of them affect you.

1 **Overproduction.** This means creating too much of something, particularly when producing something now for later and then not needing it. It could apply to a tangible product or a plan or a document. (See Secrets 1.2 and 1.4.)

2 **Waiting.** Having to stop and wait for something or someone to arrive so you can carry on; waiting for information; chasing other people; waiting to use a piece of equipment. (See Secrets 3.5, 3.9 and 7.4.)

3 **Unnecessary movement.** Having to travel around the workplace to go to the areas you need; having to travel to another place to see someone. (See Secret 4.7.)

4 **Over-processing.** Spending more time than is necessary doing something, such as putting unnecessary detail into paperwork. Spending hours in a meeting that could have taken half the time. (See Secrets 1.2, 2.3 and 4.5.)

5 **Searching.** Looking for something that would have been easy to find if it had been stored or filed sensibly. (See Secret 4.7.)

6 **Distraction.** Being distracted from tasks in hand by something else – smoke break, someone's holiday photos, answering the phone for absent colleagues, attending a meeting in which you don't need to participate. (See Secrets 4.1, 4.2 and 4.5.)

7 **Getting it 'wrong'.** An example would be not knowing how to set up a spreadsheet and therefore taking three times as long to do the same job on, say, a Word table using a calculator to generate the numbers (or not realizing that Word tables themselves have a formula function!). Or not having an adequate or accurate brief and therefore producing something that doesn't fulfil the desired objective (see Secret 1.2).

Think about the things that frustrated you today about not getting things done, and see which of the Seven Wastes were involved.

4.5

Manage your meetings

The higher up the corporate ladder you climb, the more time you will spend in meetings. The more time you waste in meetings that are badly run or meetings that you don't even need to be in, the less you get done!

To **arrange** a meeting effectively:

■ Only invite people who need to contribute to the meeting.
■ Set a specific objective for the meeting. For example, 'Meeting to set next year's prices', rather than 'Meeting to consider next year's prices'. 'Meeting to decide our response to the complaint from X Ltd', rather than 'Meeting about the complaint from X Ltd'.
■ Clarify the overall time allotted for the meeting. For example, '10am to 11am' rather than just '10am'.
■ Send out agendas well in advance so people know what is expected of them.
■ For more complex meetings, allot a specific person's responsibility and an amount of time to each issue:

Meeting to set next year's prices

Subject	Person	Time (start 10am)
Competitor pricing	Sam Ng	15 minutes (to10.15)
Market conditions	Jo Patel	15 minutes (to 10.30)
Product cost forecast	Chris Ndumba	10 minutes (to 10.40)
Sales forecast	Tosh McIntosh	10 minutes (to 10.50)
Discussion	All	20 minutes (to 11.10)
Vote	All	5 minutes (to 11.15)
Summary of decisions	Tosh McIntosh	10 minutes (to 11.25)

To **manage** a meeting effectively:

- Start on time.
- Control use of time; prevent unnecessary discussion.
- Manage questions and answers in discussion sessions.
- Focus people on the objective and manage your voting system (if you are having one).
- Summarize outcomes and next actions clearly.

To **contribute** effectively to a meeting:

- Only attend if you need to.
- Know what is expected of you and prepare in advance.
- Stay focused on the objective.

Badly managed meetings stop you doing more useful things.

4.6

Fight fatigue

Fatigue can stop you getting things done and it can also be an effect of poor time management: "It takes so long and I work so hard to get my job done that I'm constantly exhausted." We can look at fatigue in this context in two ways: how to avoid fatigue and how to fight fatigue when you're tired.

How to avoid fatigue

■ **Vary your routine.** Do something different.
■ **Avoid simple carbohydrates.** Sugar causes blood sugar levels to spike. After eating sugar, your body releases insulin, which makes you tired.
■ **Eat complex carbohydrates.** Food that breaks down slowly is better – health bars, bagels and pasta.
■ **Check your iron levels.** Eat fish, eggs, chicken, fortified cereals and beans.
■ **Go to bed at the same time every night.** The time you go to bed is more important than the time you get up.

How to fight fatigue when you are tired

Get moving. The more oxygen in you, the more energized you'll feel. Exercise releases hormones that make you feel refreshed.

Eat dark chocolate! It contains antioxidants that are better than vitamin C at limiting fatty deposits in the brain and heart.

Splash yourself with cold water.

Expose yourself to bright light. Preferably natural daylight.

Make fists with your feet. This is a method for overcoming jet-lag. Slip your shoes off under your desk and bunch your toes.

Use your sense of smell. Strong scent can make you more alert very quickly; think 'smelling salts'! For example, peppermint can lower fatigue by 15% and increase alertness by 30%.

The smell of coffee also works. Simply smelling coffee can awaken a person.

Massage key areas. The top of your head, the back of your neck and the back of your hands.

A little caffeine can help a lot. Making a cup of tea or coffee will get you up and provide some caffeine to perk you up as well.

Listen to music that's energizing to you.

Eat fruit. It will perk you up in a healthy way

Drink ice cold water. The coldness picks you up, and you'll get up regularly to visit the toilet.

Brush your teeth.

Fatigue can be dangerous as well as reducing your effectiveness. Learn to avoid and fight fatigue.

4.7

Practise 'good housekeeping'

In this instance we are talking about the policy of keeping 'a place for everything and everything in its place'. This is a massive timesaver that helps you to have the right things easily available in order to allow you to get things done.

'Good housekeeping' is a tool from the Quality, Excellence and Lean movements in the manufacturing sector. It is a simple and effective way to reduce waste and therefore wasted time, and it is just as relevant in the office or even in the home. It follows the five-step, five-'**S**'es process:

1   **Sort.** Get rid of all the clutter by identifying what you need and only keeping that. For instance, if you have to fill in a particular paper form twice a day, keep copies of that, but get rid of all the old marketing literature in the same drawer. In this sorting stage also identify the quantities you need to keep to hand. If you use 2oz of sugar per day, there is no point in keeping a 50lb sack in the kitchen.

2 **Segregate.** Arrange things logically in relation to where they are needed. For instance, in a workshop keep everyday hand tools right next to the workbench, whilst once-a-week stuff can be in the storeroom across the yard.

3 **Shine.** Make sure everything works properly and is fully loaded. For instance, if the knife is blunt, sharpen it. Check that there are staples in the stapler.

4 **Strengthen.** Create methods, habits or policies to keep things cleared out, configured and clean. This might include labelling drawers, colour coding things, shadow boards, putting 'do not remove' labels on tools, files and equipment.

5 **Standardize.** Stick to the conformity. Don't backslide into old habits such as leaving the filing until the end of the month, not washing the cups at the end of each day. On a personal basis this means getting into a good habit. On a team basis it means making it a rule and enforcing that rule.

Have a place for everything and keep everything in its place.

4.8

Avoid procrastination

Procrastination is the act of putting off until tomorrow that which you ought to do today. There are many reasons for procrastination but we are all guilty of it to some degree or another. The dangers of procrastination are many and varied and for that reason we must avoid it and get things done.

If you find yourself carrying the same item over on your 'to do' list day after day, getting into trouble because you haven't done something that you knew you should have done, discovering last-minute problems that last an hour, or finding that your 'to do' list gets longer as you get nearer to the deadlines, then you are probably procrastinating!

The dangers of procrastination are that you run out of time to get really important things done because you didn't start early enough. You become the bottleneck and everyone else hates you for it and you get nagged and micro-managed because you have failed to fulfil promises or expectations.

Procrastination is self-perpetuating. If you haven't done thing A, thing B is held up and they both take longer to do than they should. This in turn holds up things C and D and so on.

"Hard work is often easy work that did not get done at the proper time" Bernard Meltzer, American radio host

You probably procrastinate on jobs you don't like doing. "This is a big job", you tell yourself, "and I have little spare time". This is perhaps a job you don't see the point of. You may be worried that you'll mess it up, so putting it off puts off the point of possible failure. Perhaps you procrastinate because you know that the longer you put something off, the more likely it is that someone else will decide to do it for you. You might even be trying to fool people that you are overworked!

Ways to avoid procrastination:

- Stop putting things on your 'to do' list without justification!
- Ask someone else to do it for you.
- Try to find a quicker, better or more guaranteed way to do it.
- Break it down into smaller parts and do it bit by bit.
- Find out why it is important.
- Clarify your goals and milestones.
- Make a deal with yourself about a 'reward' for doing it. (Secret 4.2.)
- Be honest with yourself about your workloads.

Don't procrastinate, get on and do it!

4.9

'Sharpen the saw'

OK, now you are really wondering what I'm talking about: 'sharpen the saw'? There is a book entitled *The 7 Habits of Highly Effective People* (see further reading) – one of those habits is referred to as 'sharpening the saw'.

The story goes like this:

Two pairs of lumberjacks are working in the forest cutting down trees with big, two-man handsaws. The first pair start at 9am and do nothing all day but cut down trees; they don't stop sawing except to run from one tree to the next. It takes them 20 minutes to cut down

case study Kate worked in a busy marketing department. Her workload kept increasing to the point that she was not getting everything done in 12-hour days without a single break. Her boss, Carl, didn't seem to notice how hard she was working. She was exhausted and told the human resources manager, Sue, that she felt like resigning. Sue spoke with Kate's boss and found that Carl did not consider that he was giving

e first tree, 30 minutes for the second, 45 for the third, 1 hour for the urth and so on. This is because their saw is getting blunter as the day es on and they are getting more tired. By the end of the working day ey have cut down 9 trees. They stay late to sharpen the saw ready for morrow and finally go home, where they are too tired to spend quality ne with their families.

The second pair start at 9am and also take 20 minutes to cut wn their first tree. Then one makes some tea and the other sharpens e saw; this takes 10 minutes. It then takes them 20 minutes to cut wn the second tree. Then one sharpens the saw whilst the other akes the tea. It then takes them 20 minutes to cut down the third ee. They repeat this process throughout the day. By the end of the orking day they have cut down 14 trees, had an hour for lunch and arpened the saw ready for tomorrow. They have taken plenty of reathers' during the day, so they go home with enough energy left to end time with their families and have a 'life'.

The moral of the story is to pace yourself and keep looking wards the future, rather than just going at it without a break. You will t more done and have a better work/life balance.

on't forget to 'sharpen the saw' on a egular basis.

ate an excessive workload compared with other staff, nly that Kate was very disorganized – but he hadn't been elping Kate to organize the workload more efficiently, nd had not realized the long hours she was doing. The three f them sat down together and worked out ways of eorganizing Kate's working day, which included Kate aking regular breaks, keeping an updated 'to do' list, nd Carl giving her better guidance.

Saying "no"

You have done all the things laid out in the earlier chapters of this book and you would be able to get everything done if only people would stop coming and asking you to do even more things. You need to learn to say "no", but you need to find ways that don't sound so rude or negative as a straight "no". This short chapter will help you learn to say "yes... if" or "no... because" – two assertive and constructive ways to ensure you stay on top of that workload.

5.1

Don't say "yes" to every request

Many of us find it really hard to say "no", especially to our manager, our parents or our spouse. However, if we say "yes" to every request, one of two things will happen: either we will end up working 24 hours a day or we will end up letting people down because we said "yes" to something we cannot do.

If you find saying "no" difficult, here is a way of making it easier.

■ When you feel the need to say "no" but the duty to say "yes", try saying "yes, if…" instead.

■ So, if you have been asked to attend a meeting but you have a full schedule of things to do, try saying: "Yes, I'll attend the meeting if you can arrange with my manager that I can have an extra day to complete the monthly report."

Alternatively you can use: "Yes, I'll attend the meeting, if you can tell me which of these tasks you are happy not to have done."

"Yes, if…" sounds much better than "No, because I'm too busy". If, however, you are concerned that the person will hear only the "yes" because it comes at the beginning of the reply, you can use: "If… then yes" instead.

So you might say: "If you can allow me not to finish these drawings until tomorrow, then yes, I can attend that meeting."

'Yes... if" is an appropriate response for a genuinely busy person.

5.2

Just say "no"

Some people have been brought up to be always helpful, and certainly at work a 'can do' approach is generally encouraged. Unfortunately, this might lead you to realize that you have said "yes" to everything you were asked to do and now can't get everything done even if you were to work 24/7.

If you are working within an industry that provides written job descriptions or key performance indicators, then you will probably be obliged to say "yes" to the tasks that fall within those remits. If you are asked to do something that is outside that job description – or certainly if it is a favour for someone – then you have a right (and possibly even a responsibility) to say "no".

case study You should simply say "no" when your health is at stake, but some people have difficulty recognizing this. William took on long shifts as a forklift truck operator to support his wife and young children. He ignored the fact that his hands were shaking – compromizing the safety of himself and others at work

Say "no" if, by saying "yes", you:

Would be failing to do something else important to you.

Would be taking on a task you cannot do because of a lack of skill or knowledge.

Would be committing to a promise you cannot keep because you simply cannot do it in the time available.

Would be put under unacceptable personal strain, such as the inability to spend time with your family, or because it would compromize your health.

Would be committing others (for example your family) without their acceptance.

When you have to say "no" in situations like these, take the **NB** approach: **N = "No".** Say the actual word "no"; say it clearly and leave a pause so the other person really hears it. **B = "Because..."** Explain the reasoning behind your refusal. Most people will accept "no" when they can see a sound justification and unpleasant consequences (for you or more especially them!)

As in Secret 5.1, you may prefer to turn it the other way round and say "Because... No".

Sometimes you have a responsibility to say "no"; it is more professional than saying "yes" and then failing.

and that his health was deteriorating. Eventually, he was diagnosed with a disease of the nervous system. He was surprised to find that his family and boss were very supportive once he admitted the problem, and he was offered an alternative job that did not involve operating machinery.

5.3

Use 5Y questioning

You may well be able to use the 5Y questioning technique to get people to decide not to ask *you* to do something but to do it themselves or ask someone else! The 5Y technique comes from 'cause and effect analysis', but is a useful technique for anyone who has many demands and requests made of them.

'5Y' stands for 'Five Whys' – an easy way to remember to ask five levels of question to get to the underlying purpose or cause of something. You can use it to question someone about why they are asking you to do something, and get to the crux of the matter. You don't literally need to ask "why?" five times – it's working through five levels of questioning that's important.

For example:
"John, please get me the sales figures for the automotive industry last quarter."
"May I ask what you want them for?" *(Level 1)*
"I need to use them to project sales for the next quarter."
"How much detail do you need? Overall figures or broken down by manufacturer?" *(Level 2)*

"Er, broken down by manufacturer, I guess."

"Do you want them also broken down by region?" *(Level 3)*

"Um, yes, that would be good."

"And by product and month?" *(Level 4)*

"Yes, I suppose I do!"

"When do you need the information?" *(Level 5)*

"I have to submit my report by the 25th, so I suppose the 21st when I need you to give me the information."

(You now have all the information you need to say…) "Well, I have to get this other monthly plan completed and delivered on the 20th, so if you want the sales figures, then…"

"…I'll have to ask you to speak to the other manager who I do the monthly plan for and see if he will accept his plan being late this month."

"…you would probably be better off asking someone else to do it."

"…you can see that I won't be able to do them by the 21st; how about the 23rd?"

Note that all five levels of questioning here were closed questions, which allowed John to keep control of the conversation.

Often just by asking sensible questions you can persuade someone to refine or simplify their request.

Dealing with problems

This chapter will help you to avoid problems by assessing and managing risks. If something has already gone wrong, then you are given tools to help you understand the root causes of the problem and to work out a logical solution. You will be encouraged to think about both quick, short-term fixes and long-term solutions that stop a problem recurring. Included are stories that show how you can improvise with cheap and quick solutions when time is limited.

6.1

Assess risks sensibly

Whenever you put something on a 'to do' list, there is always a risk that something will cause it to go wrong. Therefore, you have to carry out some form of risk assessment to give you the best possible chance of it going right.

Risk Assessment is a tool from project management methods such as PRINCE2™. In that context it is a 'heavy' tool, but its principles are just as sound for smaller, everyday tasks, as they are to long projects. It is a good idea simply to ask a couple of questions about each item on your list so that you have at least consciously considered the risks rather than been blissfully ignorant of the possibility of a risk.

There are three questions that you need to ask: What could stop me from doing this task on time? How likely is it that this will occur? What would be the impact on the task/time if it occurs?

For example: I have an item on my 'to do' list, which is 'Write next chapter of the Getting Things Done book'.

What could stop me?
■ Other things could distract me.
■ My PC could crash.
■ I might not be able to find the reference works I need.

How likely are these things to occur?

■ It is very likely that I could be distracted, especially by the telephone.
■ It is unlikely that the PC will crash today; it hasn't crashed for months.
■ It is very unlikely that I won't be able to find the reference works because they are in a box by my desk and I used them yesterday.

What would be the impact if any of these things did occur?

■ Being distracted by other people would have a major impact because I have to meet a deadline for submitting the work.
■ My PC crashing would have a very high impact, because I'd have to fix the PC and possibly lose the work I've already done.
■ Not finding my reference works would have relatively little impact because I know most of the material already.

These answers could be represented graphically as

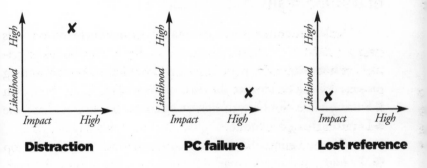

Distraction   **PC failure**   **Lost reference**

Now that you have assessed the risks sensibly you can go on to manage those risks; this is covered in Secret 6.2.

Work out the likelihood of various things happening to delay you, and the level of impact if they occur.

6.2

Manage risks well

In Secret 6.1 we looked at assessing risks sensibly. Once you have assessed the risks you are then able to manage them – in other words, to make a considered plan to ignore, reduce the likelihood or control the impact if any risk becomes a reality.

Using the same example of risks that we used in Secret 6.1:

Distraction was high impact and high likelihood. We must manage this risk and reduce the *likelihood* by:

■ Putting a 'Do Not Disturb' sign on our office door.
■ Diverting our desk phone.
■ Switching off our mobile.
■ Not logging on to our email.

We can control the *impact* of the risk by:

■ Starting the task with enough time to allow for some delays. (If the task takes an hour and we have to complete by 11am, then we should start at 9.30am.)
■ Asking for an extension of the deadline for the task.
■ Asking for a reduction in the quality standard for the task. For instance, a draft of a document rather than a finished document.

one minute wonder Contingency plans are always worth considering. You keep spare light bulbs under the sink as a contingency plan against the risk of bulbs failing. An airliner has a battery-powered automatic back-up lighting system as a contingency plan for a power failure in the dark.

PC failure was high impact but low likelihood. We might choose to reduce only the *impact* of this risk as it is so unlikely to happen. It will depend on the relative cost of the management solution.
■ If we have a second PC/laptop, we could charge it (a contingency plan), but we probably wouldn't go out and buy a back-up machine.
■ We should take low-cost precautions, such as making frequent saves of our work and copying it onto a disc or data stick, printing off the work to date, or emailing it to a colleague/home mailbox regularly.

Lost reference was a risk that was low impact and low likelihood. We would probably choose to ignore this risk altogether.

The important thing is to decide what to do about the risk in advance, rather than having something go wrong and saying, "Oh, dear! I never thought that would happen!"

Assessing and managing risk makes it more likely that you will get everything done on time.

6.3

Define problems

You need to be quite sure that you have defined what the 'problem' is before you try to solve it; otherwise you may spend a lot of time finding a 'wrong' solution, and that is going to prevent you from getting a lot of other things done.

We need to be very careful to define the problem rather than jump to a half solution. Here is a story to illustrate this point.

■ **The objective.** The government of a small country wanted to build an observation post on top of an isolated mountain.

■ **The situation.** The sides of the mountain were very steep and heavily forested. The slopes were almost solid rock with a lot of ravines. The existing highway was half a mile from the foot of the mountain and about 1,500 feet lower than the spot they had selected for the observation post.

Money was tight: the government had a very limited budget for this project; certainly not enough to fund the construction of an access road in such difficult terrain. Whilst a helicopter pad could be built on the summit, the cost of getting the material there by helicopter was

> "If we can really understand the problem, then the answer will come out of it, because the answer is not separate from the problem" **Jiddu Krishnamurti, Indian philosopher**

prohibitive. The ongoing commitment to supplying the post monthly by helicopter was unacceptable.

The problem. The problem was initially talked about in terms of the difficulties of building a robust and lasting road within a very limited budget. The road engineers struggled with the problem, and discussions continued for weeks because no-one could work out how to build a good road very cheaply. One day, someone suddenly took a broader viewpoint and said: "So how *do* you get a couple of tons of material up a mountain, in a way that is repeatable?" The problem was now actually defined better, and the solution almost leapt off the paper...

The solution... A cable car! The materials to build a tower at the summit were taken by helicopter, which was then not needed again. A level track was made to the foot of the mountain, where another tower was constructed. The cable was hoisted over all the ravines, rocks and trees. It was affordable and there was no need for a road at all.

You can't start to solve a problem successfully until you really know what the problem really is.

6.4

'Appreciate' problems

An 'appreciation' of a problem is a logical thought process. It begins by identifying the objective you must achieve to overcome the problem and ends with a plan to implement. By following a set process, you view the issue more comprehensively.

1 An appreciation begins with the definition of your goal or objective. This is linked inextricably to the problem that you have, but be sure to learn the lessons of Secret 6.3.

2 Next you need to consider all the factors in the current situation that might affect whether you achieve that objective. The factors will be different, depending on the situation. For example in business you may use the PESTLE factors (Secret 2.3). For each factor, state the fact and then ask, "so what?".

Fact: the mountainside has deep ravines. *So what?* Vehicles cannot cross ravines so we would have to level the ground. *So what?* Levelling the ground on a remote mountain is very costly. *So what?* We have only a small budget so we can't level the ground. (As you can see there will be lots of "so whats?")

Consideration of the factors will highlight options that won't work. Now we have to consider the options that are left and compare the merits of each. The criteria you use to compare options depend on your situation, but broadly they will fall into the areas of cost versus benefit. These may be financial costs and benefits or they could include personal injury as a cost, or the feeling that you are doing something as a benefit.

At this point you might realize that your original objective is hopelessly unattainable and you may need to go back and start again. (This isn't as bad as it sounds because much of the appreciation of factors and options will still be relevant.)

3 Once you have identified your objective, considered all the factors and compared the options open to you, you now have to pick one of the options and make that into your plan. The 'right' option may be anything from a very obvious, easy solution through to choosing from options with similar cost/benefit outcomes. You will have to make a choice, and that is a judgement call that only you can make. You will find that the appreciation you have already done will help you on the detailed planning as well as helping you to 'sell' the solution to others.

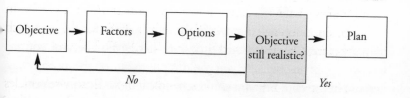

Appreciating the problem brings benefits beyond the solution itself.

6.5

Choose a quick fix, then a long fix

Problems stop you from getting things done. You can often solve a problem with a 'quick fix' and get on with the rest of the 'to do' list. What you then need to do is consider a long fix in order to stop the problem from recurring and delaying you again.

Getting a problem fixed for today is called a 'band-aid' approach, and it is a good way of getting things done in the short term. For a lot of us, a 'band-aid' approach is all we can do because we have so much else to do each day that we cannot take the time to fix the problem long term. The environment can also prevent us, or the time may not be right for a long fix.

For instance, you discover in the rainy season that the roof leaks in many places. You haven't the time to fix it long term because you are too busy emptying buckets; you couldn't put mastic on the roof anyway because of the rain! But you could schedule it in for the dry season.

The same goes for most other problems, and, if you are a manager, it is probably part of your role to improve processes in order to increase efficiency and stop problems from recurring. If you aren't a manager, it is still worth trying to get long fixes done for two reasons:

"All mistakes are there, waiting to be made" Savielly Tartakower, chess grandmaster

■ It shows you as a person with initiative, so it can lead to promotion.

■ In any case, you are the person who will have to stop what you are doing and fix the problem when it recurs!

You can carry out a long fix on a problem using the secrets in this book. First, define the problem, do a root cause analysis, appreciate the problem, improvise if appropriate, schedule tasks needed for a long fix, involve others where appropriate by managing meetings, influencing, giving instructions and saying thanks.

Two things to remember about long fixes:

■ You may have a problem that was a one-off; it isn't going to recur. Therefore, trying to impose a long fix is going to be a waste of time. Root cause analysis will tell you if you need to go for a long fix or not.

■ Implementing a long fix is seldom regarded as a priority until the problem recurs. This means that the job of fixing is often forgotten, so put it into your 'to do' list or diary.

Doing a long fix shows that you learn from experience; not doing a long fix suggests that you don't.

6.6

Find the root cause

When something goes wrong and you want to consider a long fix to stop it happening again, it is really, really important to find the root cause of the problem. If you don't find it, you end up treating the symptom, not the problem itself.

To find the root cause of a problem you will have to ask lots of questions. You have to check all possible areas that could be contributing to a problem, rather than making assumptions about the first element of a problem that you identify.

To help with this there is a tool called an **Ishikawa diagram**. This gives you a series of areas in which to ask questions, to discover all the factors that may be feeding into the problem.

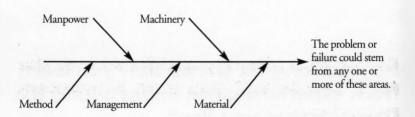

Manpower   Machinery

The problem or failure could stem from any one or more of these areas.

Method   Management   Material

"In business, as in medicine, treatment without diagnosis is malpractice!" Alan Taylor, businessman

You may want to think of areas that are more relevant to your problem but for most people the **5 Ms** – manpower, machinery, method, management and material – work well.

For example, let's say that the problem is your vehicle running out of fuel. You have refilled it and therefore fixed the short-term problem and completed your journey. Now you want to make sure that running out of fuel doesn't stop you from doing your job in the future. So you need to ask some questions.

■ **Manpower.** Whose job is it to fill the vehicle? Do they know it is their job? Are they doing it?
■ **Machinery.** Is the vehicle leaking fuel? Is the fuel gauge working properly? Is the fuel pump delivering the displayed amount of fuel?
■ **Method.** Is the person whose job it is to fill the vehicle putting the fuel in the right place? Is the driver driving in a way that uses up more fuel than it should?
■ **Management.** Are we able to afford enough fuel? Is the fuel available in the right place?
■ **Material.** Are we using the right type of fuel?

Only if you identify and fix ALL of the root causes will you stop a problem recurring.

6.7

Learn how to improvise

Improvisation – which is the creative use of alternative materials and methods – is a perfectly legitimate tactic to adopt for solving a problem. You can improvise to create a quick fix; sometimes an improvised method provides an excellent long-term solution that no-one had considered before.

The main skill in improvising effectively is to think laterally, and many people are naturally good at this. In developing nations, improvisation is a way of life; it is in the industrialized world that people have become dependent on modern technology, specialist products and specialist people.

You can train yourself to think laterally in the following ways:
■ Deliberately try to solve problems by improvising a solution.
■ Imagine problems and try to think of improvised solutions. "How could I fix X if I didn't have the 'proper' tools or parts?"
■ Make an effort to learn how things and processes work; this breaks things down into component parts, making it easier to find an improvised solution.

Here are some examples of historical improvisations that may inspire you.

■ Adapting what is available to replace something missing.
Early in the 20th century, the members of an ill-fated Arctic expedition were in desperate need of rescue but their radio was damaged. The broken component was a resistor; someone asked what a resistor was made of, and the answer was "carbon". He replaced the broken resistor with a small piece of paper covered with pencil strokes. It worked!

Another example: when rationing was rife in Britain during and after World War II, housewives were unable to get pineapples, but swedes and turnips were abundant. They cut these into small chunks and soaked them in sugar solution for 'pineapple' recipes.

■ Using what you are stuck with to fix a new problem. In 1947, faced with a declining market for their product, Debs Silk Protector, the Deb Company discovered that the product was also good at removing grease and grime from skin. They re-branded the product as Swarfega and targeted people working in grimy environments, such as mechanics. Decades later Swarfega is still a top global seller.

■ Transferring a skill you possess to do something new. In 2009 Hertfordshire Police in the UK wanted to obtain really useful advice about burglary prevention; they improvised a low-cost solution by offering convicted burglars the opportunity to work off their sentences by acting as 'consultants'!

Any fool can spend lots of money to fix a problem; it takes a spark of genius to improvise a cheap, effective solution.

Asking others to do things

Sometimes you are best served by getting others to do things for you. However it is not always easy either to persuade others to help you or to do the task properly. In this chapter you will find secrets that help you to influence where you have no power or authority; to delegate tasks effectively; to give instructions that will maximize the likelihood of a successful outcome; and to show an appropriate level of gratitude that will encourage others to help you further.

7.1

Work to YOUR strengths

Self-awareness is a brilliant tool. If you develop an awareness of your own strengths and weaknesses, your likes and dislikes, then you can work *to* your strengths rather than *despite* your weaknesses. This will also allow you to identify the things that ideally others could help you with.

There are many tests available to help you identify your personality type, work preferences, learning styles, communication styles and technical ability. These tests range from the highly academic to the positively lightweight. You can pay a lot of money for them at the practice of a business psychologist or you can complete one in a glossy magazine. You can also simply sit and ask yourself and your close colleagues some key questions, then analyse the answers yourself.

Start off with these:
■ What am I good at in my current job?
■ How good am I at these things?
■ What do I enjoy doing?

"We can't take credit for our talents. It is how we use them that counts."

Madeleine L'Engle, American writer of young adult fiction

These are the things you should try to develop in your role and your career. If you observe other people struggling with these things, then investigate the possibility of taking on some of their work or teaching them how to do it better.

Then ask yourself:
- What am I not so good at in my current job?
- What do I hate doing?
- What effect does this have on my ability to get things done?

Assess whether these elements are an integral part of your job. If they are, then you need to try to improve your abilities. Here you might be able to learn from someone who is better at them than you. If these elements aren't integral to your role, you should see if there are other people who would be better placed/able to do them instead.

So long as you aren't limiting your long-term career by not doing things that you need to do in the future, then by following this approach and working to your strengths you will get a lot more done. By using your strengths to help others you will help them to get a lot more done as well.

Working to your strengths is about accentuating the positive and eliminating the negative.

7.2

Influence others

If you want to ask other people to do things for you but you don't have any authority or power over them, then you are going to have to influence them. Some of us are natural influencers, but influencing is a skill you can learn, even if you have never had any success in the past.

Three different areas of thought influence people:
■ Logic.
■ Credibility and recommendation.
■ Their feelings and emotions about the issue.

The logical argument presents the details and the implications; it is considered and supported by evidence at every step. For instance, "You will save $45 if you buy this printer."

An argument based on credibility and recommendation relies more heavily upon the qualifications and the status of its supporters. For instance, "This laptop is made by a top Japanese firm and the President uses one."

Sometimes we are influenced by our emotions and feelings. For instance, "Owning this satellite navigation system will give you the confidence you want."

Different people will 'weight' these areas differently. For example, some people will be swayed by a very logical argument whilst others are more emotional. Some will always do what a 'credible' person suggests, whilst others will demand to see every logical reason before rejecting the argument because they don't view its proponent as credible.

You should use a WIIFY approach, which is the same as a WIIFM ('What's In It for Me', see Secret 1.9) idea, turned into a 'What's In It For You' persuasion device:

■ **Influencing the other person by stressing the area you know they tend towards: logic, credibility or emotion.** If you don't know how this person leans in this environment, then you'll need to take a more wide-ranging approach.

■ **Producing a balanced argument that combines all three areas.** "If you do this for me it'll skill you up for your next promotion; I know that your boss will want you to learn to do this sometime soon, and besides, won't you feel good when you deliver it to the customer!"

If your attempt to influence someone isn't successful first time, try again; sometimes you have to assert yourself and show that you are serious about the matter.

Logical argument alone is seldom enough. Humans have feelings and are swayed by the opinions of others.

7.3

Give good instructions

There is nothing as frustrating as managing to persuade someone to do something for you and then having to redo it because they did it 'wrong'. Often this happens not because they were incompetent but because you didn't give good instructions!

Secret 1.2 was about asking others for clear instructions so that you can get things done properly for others. Likewise, if you want others to do things properly for you, then you have to give them instructions that cannot be misinterpreted.

You may already know the mnemonic **SMART**:

■ **S = Specific.** Ensure that your instruction is specific. "Press your shirt and polish your shoes" is a more specific instruction than "smarten yourself up". Beware using ambiguous words; if you want someone to sell something, don't say "market it" or "dispose of it", say "sell it".

■ **M = Measurable.** Make your instruction as measurable as possible. "Please buy me an exterior door, 190cm by 100cm for no more than $35," is more measurable than "please buy me a door".

■ **A = Achievable.** Be very comfortable in your own mind that the person you are asking to do this task has both the ability and the willingness to complete it. If they don't really have the ability then they will probably fail and that is damaging to all. If they haven't got the willingness then you are going to have to supervise, chase and check to ensure the job is done properly. In that case it may be quicker to do the job yourself!

■ **R = Relevant.** The task must be relevant to the person doing it: either relevant to their job or relevant to them personally. If it isn't, then you will be held responsible for distracting them from their real job, or they might rightly question why they should do it for you at all.

■ **T = Timebound.** When you set a time for completion be as precise as possible: "By 5pm on Friday the 31st of July" rather than "by the end of the week".

If you google "SMART Objectives" you will find that many organizations use a version of this mnemonic to suit their management style. One researcher counted 1,700 interpretations of SMART.

Take five minutes to give good instructions, otherwise you'll be taking much longer to redo a task.

7.4

Learn the art of delegating

If you are a manager, team leader, supervisor or foreman, then you will have to delegate work to others. Delegating is a fundamental skill of management but it is also one that many of us find very difficult to adopt. We either want to retain control of things being done or we feel uncomfortable 'dumping' work on others.

The more you delegate, the more time you will have to manage people, manage your boss, improve processes and solve problems. In order to delegate effectively you need to ensure that the person to whom you delegate a task is provided with four things: Skill, Time, Authority and Responsibility – the **STAR** essentials.

1 **S = Skill.** You need to ensure that the person has the skill and ability to do the task; this doesn't mean that they have to be as

one minute wonder Always give someone a STAR when you delegate to them.

"Delegating work works, provided the one delegating works, too" **Robert Half, recruitment specialist**

good at it as you because you may be able to give them more time to do it than you have available.

2 **T = Time.** You need to make sure that they have adequate time in which to complete the task. If you are their manager they may be reluctant to admit that they don't have the time so try to ask open questions ("when will you do this?") rather than leading questions ("you have enough time to do this, don't you?").

3 **A = Authority.** Ensure that other people know that this person has been given the authority to complete the task. You can just tell people that they will need to provide this person with information and support or you can give them a written 'licence' or acting rank. Without the authority, the task may be much harder for them to perform.

4 **R = Responsibility.** This is often the hardest one; you are delegating something that you have a responsibility to do, but if the person you delegate to has no responsibility to you for the successful completion of the task, you alone get into trouble for their failure. One of the best ways to give the responsibility is to make it very clear that you are sharing the credit for the successful outcome.

The more you can delegate properly, the more you can get done generally.

7.5

Use WIIFYs

WIIFY is an acronym like WIIFM (Secret 1.9), but in this instance it stands for 'What's In It For You'. If you want to motivate people to do things for you, you have to 'sell' the benefits of the task – what they can personally get out of it.

Firstly with WIIFYs, you have to identify what you think are the 'benefits', not just the 'features' of a task.

For example, the 'feature' of the task of printing health and safety notices and displaying them in the workplace is that the task has to be done by law. The 'benefit' to the person is that "by doing this task you are keeping the company legal and that will be noticed and appreciated by all the bosses."

Alternatively the feature is that the person will learn a new skill, and the benefit to them is that "you will make yourself more employable, valuable and promotable."

You will notice that both of the above examples are 'positive' WIIFYs. Other positive WIIFYs might include:

■ You will be paid overtime for doing this.
■ I'll owe you a favour.

- You will enjoy it.
- There is a bonus for you for successful completion.
- It will make you feel good about yourself.
- Your confidence will improve.
- Other people will think you have already been promoted.
- Your family will benefit.
- If you do this chore for me, I'll let you do that nice job you wanted.
- It'll earn you a place in your heaven!

There are also the 'nuisance avoidance' WIIFYs. For example:

- If you do this for me I'll stop nagging you.
- By doing this you will get out of doing... (insert here something that you know they don't enjoy doing).
- The only way to keep the authorities off your back is to do this.

Sometimes people, especially where they have authority over others, forget to sell the benefits and rely on power alone to get people to do things for them. This means that the other person is not personally motivated, and you will almost certainly have to supervise, chase and check an unmotivated worker more than a motivated one, which rather defeats the object!

WIIFYs can be 'positive' or 'nuisance avoidance' – both types can help to motivate another person.

7.6

Say "thank you"

Generally human beings are motivated by recognition of their efforts and successes. Consequently, remembering to say "thank you" is a good strategy if you want people to keep doing things for you. But bear in mind that people and cultures are different, and you need to make sure that you give thanks in a way that is going to be well received.

Some people love a big, public "thank you" – a speech and a round of applause. Others find that hideously embarrassing. Picking the wrong way to say thanks does more damage than good.

Try to gauge the preference of each individual who you work with. You can even ask people what kind of show of gratitude they like, then you can pick from various popular ways to say thanks.

■ Simply saying "thank you" when they deliver the completed task.
■ A private "thank you" later on that feels completely informal.
■ A token gift to say thanks; it could be anything from a chocolate bar or a doughnut to a pen or a desk toy. Interestingly, if this comes from you personally, as opposed to coming from the company, staff are generally oblivious to the low monetary value of an item. As is often said, "it's the thought that counts."

■ A short but public speech of thanks at a regular meeting.

■ A note or email to say thanks cc'd to your boss or their boss, as appropriate.

■ A 'certificate of appreciation', framed and presented to them at a special formal event.

■ A higher value gift.

If you want to give a tangible gift (as opposed to just a verbal thank you or a certificate of appreciation), you can use a process called 'planned spontaneous recognition'. It is planned because you planned it, but it is spontaneous to the recipient because they weren't expecting it. So when they find a box of chocolates on their desk with a note that says: "Thanks for doing that report, it was great!", it comes as a pleasant surprise to them.

"Thank you" usually has great value in the workplace.

7.7

Learn from doing

A great side effect of learning how to get things done is that you learn how to do things well. You may find that you enjoy doing things, that you are good at doing things, and that you have learned how to influence others to do things, too. You can learn 'intuitively' and you can learn 'intentionally'.

■ **Intuitive learning.** We all learn intuitively simply by repetition and experience. If you hit your thumb with a hammer often enough you will learn to move your thumb before you start the downswing! The good thing about learning intuitively is that ultimately we form a habit that is almost impossible to forget. The bad thing is that it takes a long time and a lot of repetition before we get good at it.

■ **Intentional learning.** We can all learn intentionally by following a simple 'learning cycle':

1 **Do something.** You may have planned it or you may have just got on and done it.

> "Experience is not what happens to a man; it is what a man does with what happens to him"

Aldous Huxley, English novelist

2 **After it is done, stop and reflect.** Review the action; analyse it by asking what went well and what didn't go so well, what was easy and what was hard. Why were you successful or why did you fail?

3 **Learn from the experience.** Finally ask yourself what you would do the same or differently if you were doing the same task or a similar task in the future. You could also get feedback from others as to their opinions of these questions.

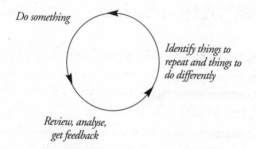

Do something

Identify things to repeat and things to do differently

Review, analyse, get feedback

If we learn intentionally we tend to learn more quickly, we are also able to describe what we have learned and this in turn allows us to pass on our learning to others and help them to learn.

The facility to learn is a skill; the opportunity to learn is a gift; the willingness to learn is a choice.

Jargon buster

5Y questioning
Technique of questioning that works through layers of causes and effects to get to the underlying purpose or cause of something.

Cause and effect analysis
A tool helps to identify all the root causes of a problem.

Closed question
A type of question to which the answer is "Yes", "No" or "I don't know".
Concurrent activity
Tasks or activities that can happen at the same time in a schedule, for example assembling furniture whilst paint is drying.

Cost/benefit analysis
A way of assessing the costs of doing something in relation to the benefits of the same thing. Where the cost and benefit are in purely financial terms it is an objective comparison. Where either or both are expressed in non-financial terms the result becomes more subjective.

DREAM
Mnemonic for Delegate, Reflect or Refuse, Escalate, Action or Make Time – the options you should apply to each item that comes into your in-tray.

Escalate
In this instance this means to refer a problem up the chain of command to someone with more authority.

Hawthorne effect
The effect that makes people act differently when they know they are being watched/measured to the way they would behave if they were not under observation.

Isometric exercise
A form of exercise devised by the Canadian air force for pilots and aircrew on long flights. It allows you to exercise muscles whilst sitting or standing still.

Just In Time / JIT
An approach, especially in manufacturing and construction, designed to reduce loss and storage costs by having components and materials delivered just in time to be used rather than have them all stockpiled before starting work.

Key Performance Indicator (KPI)
A target set at the beginning of a period by which a person's performance will be measured at the end of the period.

KISS
Mnemonic for Keep it Short and Simple – a reminder to do things in the most concise, straightforward way possible.

Leading questions

A form of closed question that leads to an expected answer, or sets limits on the possible answers. For instance, "Were you at home on the night of the murder?" as opposed to "Where were you on the night of the 17th of August?"

Mnemonic

A memory-aiding tool of a relevant word or short phrase, the letters of which spell out the initial letters of something we want to remember. For example, SMART = Specific, Measurable, Achievable, Relevant, Timebound.

Open question

Type of question that leaves the person free to select any answer, e.g. "What went wrong?" Sometimes open questions can be delivered as instructions e.g. "Tell me what went wrong?"

Output

The end result, the finished article.

Power nap

A short rest or sleep designed to boost short-term energy.

PRINCE2™

Projects in Controlled Environments – a framework for developing projects.

Prioritizing

Arranging things in order of importance. Decisions about importance will depend on the urgence, effort required and pay-off of each task.

Project management method

A formal discipline for managing projects. The most widely recognized method is PRINCE™ (PRojects IN a Controlled Environment).

Task dependency

The relationship of different tasks to each other in terms of scheduling.

'To do' list / task list

A daily list you make of all the tasks that need to be done.

WIIFM

An acronym standing for What's In It For Me? – a self-motivating factor that gives doing something a point.

WIIFY

An acronym standing for What's In It For You – something that will motivate someone else to do something for you.

Getting Things Done **secrets**

Further reading

Resources from the author

Rus Slater offers blended learning solutions
as well as traditional training interventions
and management coaching. More details
can be found at his website,
www.coach-and-courses.com

Negotiation and Influencing
An E-book by Rus Slater available to pur-
chase by download from www.coach-and-
courses.com online shop.

Mapping and Improving Processes
An E-book by Rus Slater available to pur-
chase by download from www.coach-and-
courses.com online shop.

"Too Tired?"
A free resource by Rus Slater available from
www.coach-and-courses.com,
downloadable resources page.

"Yeah, but no, but yeah"
A free resource by Rus Slater available from
www.coach-and-courses.com,
downloadable resources page.

"Time Bandits"
A free resource by Rus Slater available from
www.coach-and-courses.com,
downloadable resources page.

Publications

Allen, David *Getting Things Done: The Art of Stress Free Productivity* (Penguin) ISBN 978-0142000281

Back, Ken and Kate *Assertiveness At Work: A Practical Guide to Handling Awkward Situations* (McGraw-Hill, 2005) ISBN 978-0077114282

Covey, Stephen R. *7 Habits of Highly Effective People* (Simon & Schuster, 2004) ISBN 978 068 4858395

Evans, Clare *Time Management for Dummies* (John Wiley, 2008) ISBN 978-0470777657

Forster, Mark *Do it Tomorrow and Other Secrets of Time Management* (Hodder & Stoughton, 2006) ISBN 978-0340909126

Hemphill, Barbara *Taming the Paper Tiger at Work* (Kaplan) ISBN 978-0938721987

Reiss, Geoff *Project Management Demystified* (Taylor & Francis) ISBN 978-0415421638

Tracy, Brian *Eat That Frog! Get More of the Important Things Done, Today* (Mobius, 2004) ISBN 978-0340835043

Tracy, Brian *Goals! How to Get Everything You Want - Faster Than You Ever Thought Possible* (Berrett-Koehler, 2004) ISBN 978-1576753071

Watanabe, Ken *Problem Solving 101: A Simple Book for Smart People* (Vermilion, 2009) ISBN 978-0091929664

www.BusinessSecrets.net